Rookie
Read-About®
American
Symbols

Washington, D.C.

by Joanne Mattern

Content Consultant
Nanci R. Vargus, Ed.D.
Professor Emeritus, University of Indianapolis

Reading Consultant
Jeanne Clidas, Ph.D.
Reading Specialist

Children's Press®
An Imprint of Scholastic Inc.
New York Toronto London Auckland Sydney
Mexico City New Delhi Hong Kong
Danbury, Connecticut

Library of Congress Cataloging-in-Publication Data
Mattern, Joanne, 1963-
Washington, D.C./by Joanne Mattern.
    pages cm. — (Rookie read. About American symbols)
Includes bibliographical references and index.
ISBN 978-0-531-21569-2 (library binding: alk. paper) — ISBN 978-0-531-21842-6 (pbk.: alk. paper)
  1. Washington (D.C.)--Juvenile literature. I. Title.

F194.3.M383 2014
  975.3—dc23   2014015032

Produced by Spooky Cheetah Press
Design by Keith Plechaty

© 2015 by Scholastic Inc.

1 2 3 4 5 6 7 8 9 10 R 24 23 22 21 20 19 18 17 16 15

Photographs ©: AP Images/North Wind Picture Archives: 12, 28 right; Dreamstime: 24
(Dave Newman), 19 top left, 31 center bottom (Dinhhang), 20 top left (Jorg Hackemann),
27 (Richard Gunion), 15 (Songquan Deng), 19 top right (Sophiejames), 19 bottom (Tinnaporn
Sathapornnanont), 20 top right (Wangkun Jia); Getty Images/Central Press: 29; Jeffrey
Chandler/Art Gecko Studios: 30; Jim McMahon: 11; Media Bakery: 4 (Cade Martin), 16, 31 bottom
(Christopher Robbins); Shutterstock, Inc.: 31 top (EdBockStock), 3 top right (lesapi images),
23 (Mesut Dogan), 3 bottom (S.Borisov), 3 top left (Tribalium); Superstock, Inc.: 20 bottom
(LOOK-foto), cover (Stock Connection), 7, 28 left;

Maps p. 8 and 31 center top by XNR Productions, Inc.

Table of Contents

What Is Washington, D.C.?

Washington, D.C., is the **capital** of the United States. It is the center of our nation's government. It is also an important symbol of the United States.

Washington, D.C., contains many landmarks.

Washington, D.C., is named after George Washington, our first president. The city is home to museums, government buildings, **monuments**, and the president's house.

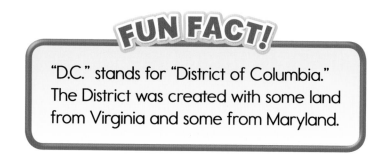

FUN FACT!

"D.C." stands for "District of Columbia." The District was created with some land from Virginia and some from Maryland.

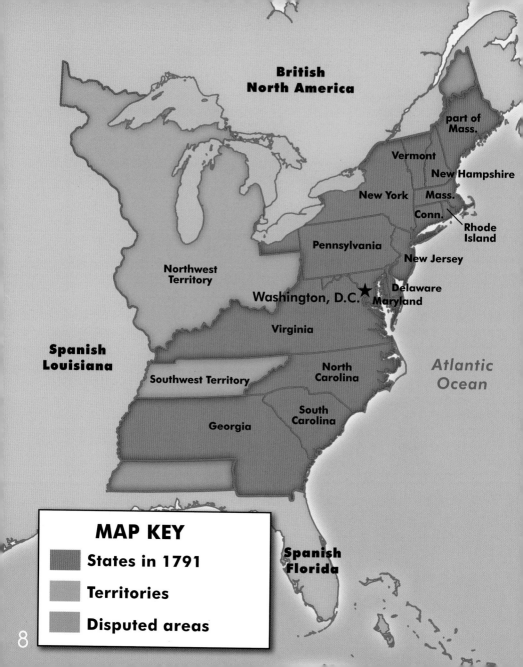

British
North America

part of
Mass.

Vermont

New Hampshire

New York   Mass.

Conn.

Rhode
Island

Pennsylvania

New Jersey

Northwest
Territory

Washington, D.C.   Delaware
Maryland

Virginia

Spanish
Louisiana

Atlantic
Ocean

Southwest Territory

North
Carolina

South
Carolina

Georgia

Spanish
Florida

MAP KEY

States in 1791

Territories

Disputed areas

Building the City

In 1791, the United States was a new country with 13 states. People wanted to have a capital city that was in the center of the country. President George Washington chose the place where the new city would be.

Washington asked French **architect** Pierre Charles L'Enfant to draw a plan for the city. Washington, D.C., became the new capital in 1800.

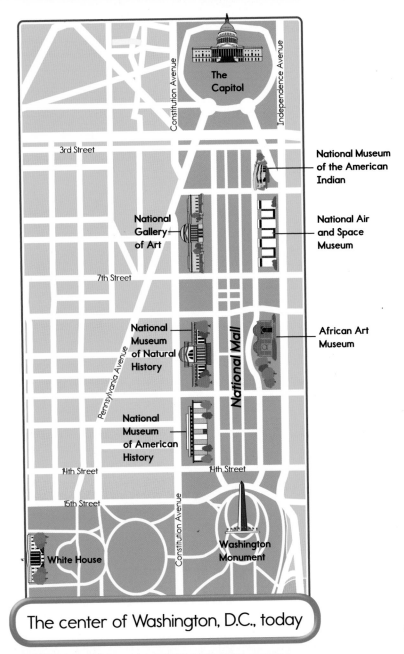

The center of Washington, D.C., today

From 1812 through 1814, the United States fought a war with Great Britain. Most of Washington, D.C., was destroyed.

After the war ended, people built the city all over again. Washington, D.C., grew even bigger and busier.

FUN FACT!

President James Madison's wife, Dolley, saved a famous painting of George Washington from being destroyed when British soldiers attacked the White House.

Many Monuments

The National Mall is an open area in the center of Washington, D.C. There are many monuments located there. The Washington Monument honors George Washington. Visitors can ride an elevator to the top.

The Washington Monument is more than 555 feet (169 meters) tall. It is made from more than 36,000 stones.

IN THIS TEMPLE
AS IN THE HEARTS OF THE PEOPLE
FOR WHOM HE SAVED THE UNION
THE MEMORY OF ABRAHAM LINCOLN
IS ENSHRINED FOREVER

The Lincoln **Memorial** honors America's 16th president. The statue of Lincoln is 19 feet (6 meters) high! When the Lincoln Memorial was built, there were 36 U.S. states. The outside of the memorial has 36 columns, one for each of those states.

Abraham Lincoln is considered one of America's greatest presidents.

Other monuments honor people who fought in wars. They help us remember the people who fought for our country.

American heroes like Dr. Martin Luther King Jr. have special monuments, too.

Vietnam Veterans Memorial

Martin Luther King Jr. Memorial

Korean War Memorial

National Air and Space Museum

National Museum of Natural History

National Museum of the American Indian

There are also many museums in Washington, D.C. These include the National Air and Space Museum, the National Museum of the American Indian, and the Museum of Natural History.

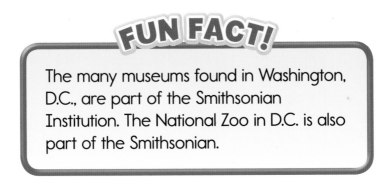

FUN FACT!

The many museums found in Washington, D.C., are part of the Smithsonian Institution. The National Zoo in D.C. is also part of the Smithsonian.

A City at Work

Washington, D.C., is the center of the U.S. government. Congress meets in the Capitol Building to pass laws.

The U.S. Capitol Building ▶

The president lives and works in the White House. There are offices downstairs where the president and his staff work. At the end of the day, the president goes upstairs. That is where he and his family live.

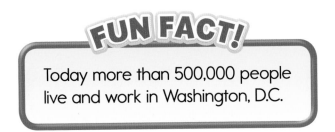

FUN FACT!

Today more than 500,000 people live and work in Washington, D.C.

More than a million people visit Washington, D.C., every year. People can visit the city's monuments, museums, and other famous places for free. Washington, D.C., invites everyone to come and learn about our country and American history.

Tourists visit the World War II Memorial. ▶

1791
President George Washington chooses the exact place where Washington, D.C., will be built.

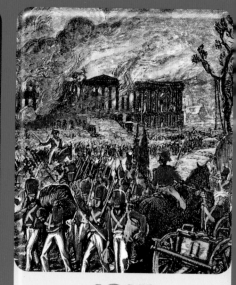

1814
British soldiers attack and burn the city during the War of 1812.

1788
Virginia and Maryland offer to give up land to be used for a new United States capital.

1800
Washington, D.C., becomes the nation's capital.

28

1963

Martin Luther King Jr. gives his famous "I Have a Dream" speech at the Lincoln Memorial.

1888

The Washington Monument opens.

1922

The Lincoln Memorial opens.

1982

The Vietnam Veterans Memorial opens.

The Capitol Building

Both the Senate and the Supreme Court used the **Old Senate Chamber** in the past. Now it's a museum.

The Senate meets in the **Senate Chamber**.

The **Rotunda** measures 96 feet (29 meters) in diameter. The top is 180 feet (55 meters) above the floor.

There are 100 statues in the **National Statuary Hall Collection**—two from each state.

The House of Representatives meets in the **House Chamber**.

Twenty-eight white marble columns line the **Hall of Columns** beneath the House Chamber.

Glossary

architect (AR-ki-tekt): person who designs buildings

capital (KAP-uh-tuhl): city where a country's government is located

memorial (muh-MOR-ee-uhl): something built to help people remember a person or an event

monuments (MON-yuh-muhnts): statues, buildings, or other structures that remind people of an event or a person

Index

Facts for Now

Visit this Scholastic Web site for more information on Washington, D.C.:
www.factsfornow.scholastic.com
Enter the keywords **Washington, D.C.**

About the Author

Joanne Mattern is the author of many books for children. She loves writing about history and its special people, places, and things. Joanne lives in New York State with her husband, four children, and numerous pets, and likes to travel as much as she can.